UNBROKEN: Sports Devotions for Injured Athletes

Biblical Guidance to Build Grit, Resilience, Perseverance & Hope for Comeback Athletes on Their Healing Journey

NextLevel Publications

Contents

WHEN INJURY CHANGES EVERYTHING

An injury does more than take you out of competition. It disrupts your rhythm, your progress, your confidence, and the way you see yourself as an athlete. Training schedules disappear. Progress feels uncertain. Waiting replaces momentum. And questions about the future can start to overshadow everything else in your life.

Most athletes are trained to compete through pressure. Very few are prepared for the mental and spiritual weight of being injured and sitting on the sidelines.

UNBROKEN: *Sports Devotions for Injured Athletes* was written for this exact season.

This devotional is for injured athletes navigating pain, surgery, rehab, long recovery timelines, and the mental battle that follows. It is for those athletes who feel frustrated by slow progress, disconnected from their team, or unsure of who they are without their sport. This book does not minimize injury or rush healing. It helps you understand what God is doing in you while your body recovers.

Inside these pages, you will walk through thirty daily devotions created specifically for injured athletes. Each devotion pairs Scripture with a real story from a professional or Olympic athlete who experienced injury, waiting, or a sidelined season. These are not exciting highlight reels or career summaries. They are honest moments that show how faith was tested, identity was challenged, and strength was rebuilt when performance was paused.

This devotional is designed to help you:

- rebuild confidence when your body feels unreliable

- separate your identity from playing time and performance

- stay mentally strong during rehab and recovery

- trust God when timelines change or answers feel unclear

- remain impactful and connected to your team, even while on the sidelines

Each daily devotion follows a simple, intentional structure to guide you through recovery with clarity and purpose:

- **Scripture Insight** that speaks directly into injury, pain, waiting, resilience, and perseverance

- **Athlete Spotlight** showing how a real athlete lived out that truth during recovery

- **Personal Reflection** to help you process emotion, doubt, and identity honestly

- **Reflection Questions** to deepen trust, faith, and perspective

- **Faith in Action** steps that turn belief into practical tasks for your daily recovery routines

- **Quiet Prayer** to steady your heart and refocus your faith

UNBROKEN is not about forcing positivity or pushing through pain. It is about rebuilding you from the inside out. Mentally. Spiritually. Emotionally. Your healing is not wasted time. God is still working on you, even when your sport is on pause. This season can strengthen your faith, shape your character, and prepare you for your big comeback.

You may feel frustrated. You may feel behind. You may feel uncertain about your future in your sport. This book is here to remind you that injury does not cancel your calling, waiting does not remove your value, and recovery does not mean you are forgotten.

You are still chosen.
You are still growing.
And you are still part of God's plan.

You may be injured, but through faith, you are **Unbroken**.

HOW TO USE THIS 30-DAY DEVOTIONAL

This devotional is designed to be read **one devotion per day for thirty days**. Each day builds on the last, helping you develop steady faith, mental strength, hope, and confidence throughout recovery. Use this book as part of your daily routine during rehab and healing. There is no need to rush ahead. What matters is showing up consistently each day and building strength, confidence, and trust over time.

1. Commit to the Process: Read one devotion each day as part of your recovery routine. Open it when you need perspective, encouragement, support, or grounding. Some days you may feel focused and hopeful. Other days you may feel tired, frustrated, or discouraged. This book is meant for all of those moments. Show up honestly, even when your energy or motivation feels low.

2. Engage Fully, Not Quickly: Each devotion is structured to help you slow down and reflect. Each Scripture speaks directly into injury, pain, disappointment, waiting, and uncertainty. The athlete story shows how their faith was lived out during recovery. Take time to think through the personal reflection and questions. Let them help you process what you are carrying physically, mentally, and emotionally. Write your answers to the reflection questions in the Journaling & Notes section at the bottom of each devotion. Growth happens when you allow truth to sink in, not when you rush to the next page.

3. Put Faith into Action: The Faith in Action steps are designed to meet you where you are right now. They are practical, realistic, and intentional. These steps help you apply faith during rehab, rest, waiting, and daily routines. Small, faithful actions repeated consistently will strengthen your mindset, rebuild confidence, and keep your focus steady throughout recovery.

4. Be Honest in Prayer: Each devotion ends with a quiet prayer to help you pause and realign your heart. Use it as a starting point, not a script. Talk honestly with God about your pain, fear, impatience, uncertainty, gratitude, and hope. God is not waiting for polished words. He is present with you in every part of this season and cares deeply about your healing.

5. Measure Growth by Faithfulness: Recovery is not linear, and neither is spiritual growth. Some days will feel productive. Others will feel slow. Do not judge progress by speed. Faithfulness matters more than perfection. If you miss a day, return without guilt. Healing and growth continue when you choose to show up again.

6. Let This Season Strengthen Others: As you move through these devotions, you may find words that resonate deeply. Share them with others close to you when appropriate. Encourage a teammate, a friend, a coach, or a family member about your progress. Your experience, perspective, and faith can impact others, even while you are healing.

CHAPTER 1: FAITH & TRUST

Leaning on God When Your on the Sidelines

1

STILL CHOSEN

"Do not fear, for I have redeemed you; I have summoned you by name; you are mine. When you pass through the waters, I will be with you, and when you pass through the rivers, they will not sweep over you."
Isaiah 43:1

Scripture Insight: Isaiah 43:1 reminds us that we are chosen by God, not by our performance or stats, but because He loves us as our Creator. God promises that He will never abandon us. He does not promise the absence of difficulty, but He promises His presence in those hard moments. Being chosen does not mean being protected from hardship. It means He will be with us even when circumstances feel confusing or painful.

Injury often strips away roles, routines, and recognition, leaving athletes questioning who they are without their sport. Isaiah 43 tells us that God's love for us is not tied to strength, speed, or talent. God still has purpose for you, even when your sport is on pause. You are still seen, still known, and still part of God's plan, even when your role looks different than you expected.

TESTED ON THE SIDELINES

Athlete Spotlight: Drew Brees once stood at a crossroads that looked like the end of his career. In the final game of the 2005 season, he suffered a devastating shoulder injury that tore his labrum and damaged his rotator cuff. Doctors and coaches questioned whether he would ever throw a football again. The team he played for chose not to bring him back, leaving his future uncertain and his confidence shaken.

For a quarterback, a throwing shoulder injury threatens the core of identity itself. Brees faced months of surgery, rehabilitation, and silence while others moved on. Without a contract, without clarity, and without guarantees of playing again, he was forced to confront who he was apart from the field. From the outside world, it looked like Brees had been passed over.

During his recovery, Brees could not control contracts, headlines, or opinions. What he could control was how he responded to his injury. He committed himself fully to rehabilitation, preparation, and his faith. He trusted that if football was part of God's plan, the door would open at the right time. And if it was not, God would still lead him forward.

That season of injury did not disqualify or remove Brees from God's plan. It redefined him. The opportunity that followed led him to a team where he would grow, lead, and make a lasting impact far beyond his statistics as a quarterback. Drew later spoke openly about how the injury strengthened his dependence on God rather than on his own abilities. His value was never erased by his injury. God carried Drew through his injury and the uncertain moments.

CHAMPION YOUR FAITH

Personal Reflection: Injury has a way of making athletes feel forgotten, replaceable, and mentally broken. Silence from coaches, reduced attention, and time away from your sport and competition can cause your purpose, identity, and confidence to feel fragile.

Reflection Questions: *What part of my purpose and identity feels threatened right now? Where do I feel overlooked, discouraged, or unsure of my place? What fears do I have about my future in my* *sport? Am I tying my value as an athlete to what I can currently do or to who God says I am?*

Faith in Action:

- Write down one fear you are carrying about your injury or future. Pray over it and release it.

- Commit to one recovery task today with excellence, even if no one notices.

- Limit comparison by taking a break from social media or team updates that stir frustration.

- Thank God specifically for one way He is present with you right now.

Quiet Prayer: God, thank You for being with me in this season, even when I feel overlooked and uncertain. Help me trust that Your calling and purpose for me have not changed because my circumstances have. Give me patience as I heal and confidence that I am still chosen by You. **Amen.**

JOURNALING & NOTES

2

TRUSTING GOD WHEN THE DIAGNOSIS HITS

"Trust in the Lord with all your heart and lean not on your own understanding; in all your ways submit to Him, and He will make your paths straight."
Proverbs 3:5–6

Scripture Insight: Proverbs 3:5–6 calls us to trust God fully, even when circumstances do not make sense. This verse does not promise understanding before obedience. It asks for trust in Him when clarity is missing. Leaning on the Lord means releasing the need to control outcomes, timelines, and explanations, especially when fear is present.

An injury diagnosis can leave athletes feeling uncertain and confused. Medical terms, test results, and recovery timelines often replace confidence with anxiety. Proverbs reminds us that God's guidance does not depend on our understanding. Even when the path forward feels unclear, God remains faithful to lead, steady, and direct those who choose trust over fear.

TESTED ON THE SIDELINES

Athlete Spotlight: Sydney McLaughlin-Levrone experienced a difficult pause in her career when extensive physical strain and fatigue forced her to step away from competition in 2022. Ongoing pain and health concerns led to medical evaluations that disrupted her training rhythm and competitive plans. For an athlete known for strict discipline, precision and control, this uncertainty replaced Sydney's confidence almost overnight.

Being sidelined challenged more than her body. Without races to anchor her identity, Sydney faced severe anxiety and pressure that training alone could not resolve. Recovery required rest, patience, and restraint, all of which felt uncomfortable for someone conditioned to push through limits. The diagnosis created questions she could not answer on her own.

Instead of forcing a return, Sydney chose to trust God with her health and future. She stepped back from competition and released control over timing and outcomes. This decision required humility, grace, and obedience, especially when expectations and public attention remained high.

That season did not weaken her faith. It strengthened it. By trusting God without full understanding, Sydney learned that obedience does not require clarity. God remained faithful through rest, recovery, and uncertainty, guiding her forward one day and one step at a time.

CHAMPION YOUR FAITH

Personal Reflection: An injury diagnosis can feel overwhelming and final. Fear often grows when answers are limited and timelines remain uncertain. Trusting God in this moment does not mean ignoring reality or pretending confidence. It means choosing where you place your trust and hope when understanding is incomplete. Like Sydney, you may be learning that strength and preparation cannot remove uncertainty. God does not ask you to see the entire path. He asks you to trust Him with your next step.

Reflection Questions: *What part of my injury diagnosis feels hardest to accept right now? Where am I tempted to rely on fear instead of trust? What unanswered questions am I holding onto tightly? How can I surrender my expectations for recovery to God?*

Faith in Action:

- Write down one medical or recovery concern that is causing fear. Pray and place it in God's hands.

- Follow today's recovery or rest plan fully, even if it feels frustrating or slow.

- Replace one anxious thought with Scripture from Proverbs 3:5-6.

- Thank God for one sign of care or support you have received during this injury season.

Quiet Prayer: God, thank You for being by my side during this setback. I admit that trusting You feels difficult when I do not fully understand what is happening in my body or future. Help me release fear and the temptations to control and place my confidence in You. Guide my steps as I heal and remind me that You are faithful even when answers are unclear. **Amen.**

JOURNALING & NOTES

3

FAITH ON THE SIDELINES

"Wait for the Lord; be strong and take heart and wait for the
Lord"
Psalm 27:14

Scripture Insight: Psalm 27:14 speaks directly to weeks of waiting that feel uncomfortable and uncertain. This verse does not describe waiting as passive or weak. It calls for strength, courage, and trust while outcomes remain unresolved. Waiting on the Lord means choosing faith when action feels limited and progress feels slow.

For injured athletes, waiting can feel like wasted time. Practices continue, games move forward, and teammates advance while recovery stalls your momentum. Psalm 27 reminds us that waiting with God still requires mental strength. Trust is not built only in motion. It is shaped in restraint, patience, and obedience when the next step is unclear.

TESTED ON THE SIDELINES

Athlete Spotlight: Tim Tebow experienced repeated seasons where opportunities disappeared without explanation. Injuries, roster changes, and shifting roles left him sidelined while younger players moved ahead. For a quarterback who thrived on competition and preparation, waiting became a defining challenge rather than a temporary setback for Tim.

Being sidelined tested more than Tebow's physical readiness. Silence from teams and limited chances to prove himself created a lot of uncertainty about his future in football. The waiting period stripped away his control and forced him to confront frustration, disappointment, and questions about his purpose and identity beyond his sport.

Instead of reacting with bitterness or panic, Tebow leaned into his faith. He committed to training, preparation, and discipline while accepting that opportunities were not guaranteed. Waiting became an active choice rooted in trust rather than fear. He focused on honoring God through his attitude, work ethic, and response to disappointment.

That season of waiting did not weaken Tebow's faith. It clarified it. By choosing patience over resentment, he demonstrated that faith is not proven only in success or visibility. Waiting on God's Plan required mental strength, courage, and humility, even when the sidelines felt long and his future felt uncertain.

CHAMPION YOUR FAITH

Personal Reflection: Waiting while injured can feel isolating and unfair. Progress may feel invisible while others continue competing. Strength in this season does not come from forcing outcomes or rushing recovery. It comes from trusting God's timing even when movement is limited and answers are delayed. Like Tim, you may be learning that faith is not measured by speed or opportunity. God remains present and purposeful even when your role feels paused and your future feels unclear.

Reflection Questions: *What part of waiting feels hardest for me right now? Where do I feel impatient or discouraged on the sidelines? What specific fears surface when progress feels slow? How can I practice trust and patience instead of frustration today?*

Faith in Action:

- Identify one area in your injury where impatience is growing and bring it honestly to God in prayer.

- Commit to today's recovery or preparation plan without rushing results.

- Encourage a teammate or peer even while you remain sidelined.

- Thank God for one way He is strengthening your character during this waiting season.

Quiet Prayer: Lord, thank You for being with me even when waiting feels difficult and uncomfortable. Give me strength and courage when progress feels slow and answers are delayed. Help me trust You with my future and remain faithful in this season. Teach me to wait with confidence, patience, and hope. **Amen.**

JOURNALING & NOTES

4

———————————

WHEN YOU DON'T UNDERSTAND THE PLAN

"For My thoughts are not your thoughts, neither are your ways My ways," declares the Lord. "As the heavens are higher than the earth, so are My ways higher than your ways and My thoughts than your thoughts."
Isaiah 55:8-9

Scripture Insight: Isaiah 55:8-9 reminds us that God's plans often operate beyond human understanding. These verses acknowledge the gap between what we expect and what God allows. They do not dismiss confusion or pain. They simply state that God's perspective is higher, broader, and more complete than our own.

For injured athletes, this truth can feel frustrating. You may do everything right and still face setbacks that make no sense. Training plans fail. Timelines change. Goals feel delayed or denied. Isaiah reminds us that just because we might not understand God's plan, does not mean He is absent in our injury or careless. Even when answers feel out of reach, God remains intentional and purposeful in what He allows and how He leads.

TESTED ON THE SIDELINES

Athlete Spotlight: In 2017 **Allyson Felix** experienced a season that challenged her understanding of success and control of her destiny. After years of dominance in sprinting, she faced physical setbacks and the strain of balancing recovery, competition, and motherhood. An Achilles injury and fatigue forced her to step back and reassess what her body could handle at that stage of her career.

For an athlete whose life had always followed a familiar competitive rhythm, this season introduced questions she could not control or predict. Recovery timelines did not always align with her expectations. Performances varied. The path forward looked different than the one Allyson had carefully mapped out earlier in her career.

Instead of forcing outcomes, Felix chose patience and trust in God. She adjusted training, honored her body, and accepted seasons where progress looked slower than expected. Her faith helped her release the need to fully understand every delay or setback. She focused on obedience and preparation rather than demanding immediate results. That willingness to trust God without full clarity sustained her through challenging seasons. Felix continued to compete with excellence, not because she understood every part of the plan, but because she trusted the One guiding it. Her story reflects the truth of Isaiah 55. God's ways often unfold differently than we imagine, yet they remain purposeful and faithful.

CHAMPION YOUR FAITH

Personal Reflection: Injury can make God's plan feel confusing and unfair. You may wonder why progress feels delayed or why recovery does not follow expectations. Not understanding does not mean you are failing in faith. It means you are human. Like Allyson, you may be learning that trust is required even when clarity is missing. God does not ask you to see the full picture. He asks you to remain faithful in the part you can see today.

Reflection Questions: *What part of my injury feels hardest to understand right now? Where am I struggling to trust God's timing? What expectations am I holding that may need to be released? In what way can I trust God even without clear answers?*

Faith in Action:

- Identify one expectation about recovery or your return to competition that may need to be surrendered to God.

- Follow today's recovery or training adjustment without resentment. Don't let rehab slide.

- Replace one frustrated thought with prayer.

- Thank God for one area of growth you are noticing through this setback.

Quiet Prayer: God, thank You for being present in my life even when I do not understand Your plan. Help me trust You when my own expectations fall short. Give me patience, humility, and hope as I heal and move forward. Teach me to remain faithful even when clarity is missing. **Amen.**

JOURNALING & NOTES

5

LETTING GO OF CONTROL

"Be still, and know that I am God."
Psalm 46:10

Scripture Insight: Psalm 46:10 calls God's people to stillness in moments of chaos and fear. This verse is not a command to stop caring or disengage from responsibility. It is an invitation to release things in your life that you cannot control and recognize God's authority. Being still requires trust and faith, especially when circumstances feel unstable or threatening.

For injured athletes, stillness can feel very uncomfortable. Injury removes control over training, performance, and timelines. Progress often depends on patience rather than effort. Psalm 46 reminds us that God remains sovereign even when we cannot act or do the things we want. Knowing God is in control does not erase difficulty, but it provides peace when strength, plans, and certainty are stripped away.

TESTED ON THE SIDELINES

Athlete Spotlight: Carson Wentz experienced a defining setback during the 2017 NFL season when he suffered a torn ACL late in the year. At the time, he was leading the Philadelphia Eagles and playing some of the best football of his career. The injury instantly removed him from competition and placed his future in uncertainty.

For a quarterback, losing physical stability impacts confidence and timing. Surgery, rehabilitation, and extended recovery forced Wentz to step away from the game while his team continued on to the Super Bowl LII without him. That timing was devasting, and the loss of control was difficult. He could not influence outcomes on the field or accelerate healing on his own terms.

During rehabilitation, Wentz faced pressure to return quickly and prove himself again. Instead of forcing recovery, he leaned into his faith and accepted the stillness required by healing. Letting go of control meant trusting God with timing, progress, and his identity beyond performance.

That season reshaped Wentz's perspective. By choosing patience and trust over urgency, he learned that faith is often strengthened when control is surrendered. The injury did not define his worth or future. It reminded him that God remains steady and present, even when circumstances remove an athlete's ability to act and perform.

CHAMPION YOUR FAITH

Personal Reflection: Injury often exposes how much control we try to maintain. You may feel restless, frustrated, or anxious when progress depends on waiting rather than effort. Letting go does not mean giving up. It means trusting God when action is limited and answers feel distant. Like Carson, you may be learning that stillness is not weakness. It is a place where faith deepens and peace begins to grow.

Reflection Questions: *Where do I feel the strongest urge to control the progress of my recovery right now? What fears surface when I am forced to slow down? In what ways can I trust God with timing instead of forcing progress? How can I practice stillness in this season?*

Faith in Action:

- Identify one area of recovery where you are pushing too hard. Consciously release it to God.

- Follow today's rehabilitation or rest plan without rushing the outcome.

- Take five quiet minutes to pray and sit in stillness without distractions.

- Thank God for one way He is caring for you during this healing process.

Quiet Prayer: Heavenly Father, thank You for supporting me even when stillness feels uncomfortable. Help me release control and trust You with my healing and my future. Give me peace as I wait and confidence that You remain in charge. Teach me to be still and rely on You. **Amen.**

JOURNALING & NOTES

CHAPTER 2: MENTAL TOUGHNESS & GRIT

Winning the Battle No One Sees

6

STRONGER THAN THE INJURY

"Therefore we do not lose heart. Though outwardly we are wasting away, yet inwardly we are being renewed day by day."
2 Corinthians 4:16

Scripture Insight: Second Corinthians 4:16 reminds believers that physical weakness does not equal spiritual decline. St. Paul acknowledges that the body can suffer, weaken, and break down, yet faith can still grow stronger. This verse speaks to the tension between what we see on the outside and what God is doing with us on the inside. Losing heart is a temptation, not a requirement.

For injured athletes, outward loss is often obvious. Strength fades, routines disappear, and confidence can feel fragile. This Scripture reminds us that healing is not limited to muscles and joints. God works inwardly during seasons of limitation. While the body recovers slowly, faith can be renewed daily through trust, patience, and dependence on God rather than performance.

TESTED ON THE SIDELINES

Athlete Spotlight: Scottie Scheffler faced ongoing physical setbacks early in his professional career that interrupted momentum and tested his patience. Minor strains and injuries affected consistency and forced him to adjust training and competition plans.

For a golfer whose success depends on consistency, precision, and rhythm, physical disruption carried mental and emotional weight for Scottie.

Golf injuries often feel isolating. Without visible physical contact or collision, bodily wear and physical strain can be misunderstood or minimized. Scheffler had to compete with uncertainty about how his body would respond under pressure. Recovery required restraint, discipline, and trust in gradual progress rather than immediate results.

Instead of forcing performance, Scheffler focused on steady preparation and faith. He acknowledged that improvement did not always show outwardly during his recovery. Progress often came quietly through rest, small adjustments, and consistent discipline. His faith helped him remain grounded when outward results lagged behind effort.

That season did not weaken Scheffler's resolve. It strengthened it. By trusting God through physical limitation, he learned that renewal does not depend on outward strength alone. God was shaping patience, humility, and endurance withing Scottie while this body healed at its own pace.

CHAMPION YOUR FAITH

Personal Reflection: Injury can make you feel as though everything is moving backward. Physical setbacks are visible and frustrating, while internal growth often goes unnoticed. This verse reminds you that renewal can still happen daily, even when progress feels slow. Like Scottie, you may be learning that strength is not only measured by what your body can do right now. God continues working in you, shaping faith, character, and resilience during recovery.

Reflection Questions: *Where do I feel most discouraged by outward setbacks right now? What signs of inner growth might I be overlooking? How does this injury challenge my definition of strength? What would it look like to trust God with daily renewal instead of immediate results?*

Faith in Action:

- Write down one way this injury has strengthened your character or perspective.

- Commit to today's recovery or training adjustment without focusing on visible results.

- Spend a few minutes thanking God for inner strength and mental toughness that is growing even if progress feels slow.

- Encourage yourself by rereading 2 Corinthians 4:16 and reflecting on its promise.

Quiet Prayer: Lord, thank You for renewing me even when my body feels weak or limited. Help me not lose heart when progress feels slow. Strengthen my faith as I heal and remind me that You are at work within me each day. Teach me to trust You through this process. **Amen.**

JOURNALING & NOTES

7

DISCIPLINE WHEN MOTIVATION IS GONE

"Do you not know that in a race all the runners run, but only one gets the prize? Run in such a way as to get the prize. Everyone who competes in the games goes into strict training. They do it to get a crown that will not last."
1 Corinthians

Scripture Insight: In 1 Corinthians 9:24–25, St. Paul compares faith to athletic training that requires discipline long after excitement fades. He reminds believers that effort matters, not for temporary rewards, but for something lasting.

Injury often drains motivation from athletes. Pain, slow progress, and repeated setbacks can make effort feel pointless. This Scripture reminds us that discipline still has value when motivation is gone. God uses consistent obedience, even in quiet or frustrating seasons, to shape endurance and character. While the physical crown fades, faith built through discipline lasts beyond recovery, competition, and performance.

TESTED ON THE SIDELINES

Athlete Spotlight: Jennie Finch faced seasons where discipline mattered more than motivation, especially as injuries and physical strain accumulated over years of elite pitching. Shoulder and knee issues required ongoing management, recovery work, and restraint. For a pitcher whose role depended on accuracy and repetition, pain and fatigue made daily training feel heavier and less rewarding.

Motivation did not always come easily during recovery periods. Long rehab sessions, limited throwing, and time away from competition tested Finch's commitment. The excitement of game days was replaced by quiet work behind the scenes. Discipline became a choice she had to make repeatedly, even when progress felt slow or unseen.

Instead of relying on emotion, Finch leaned on structure and consistency. She showed up for rehabilitation, conditioning, and preparation regardless of how she felt. Discipline anchored her when motivation faded. Her faith helped her stay focused on obedience, discipline, and responsibility rather than mood or momentum.

That discipline carried her through difficult seasons. By choosing consistency over convenience, Finch demonstrated that faith and preparation do not depend on excitement. Discipline shaped her endurance and character long before it showed up in competition. Her example reflects the truth of Scripture. Training continues because the purpose is greater than the feeling.

CHAMPION YOUR FAITH

Personal Reflection: When motivation disappears, discipline becomes the real test. Injury, fatigue, or slow progress can drain the desire to show up consistently. You may feel tempted to skip the work that no one sees or question whether effort still matters. Discipline is not about feeling driven. It is about choosing obedience when emotion is unreliable. You may be learning that steady faith and consistent effort still matter even when excitement is gone.

Reflection Questions: *Where has my motivation dropped the most during recovery or training? What responsibilities am I tempted to avoid when progress feels slow? How do I usually respond when effort feels unrewarded? How can I be more disciplined this week?*

Faith in Action:

- Identify one recovery or training habit you have been neglecting and recommit to it today.

- Set a simple, realistic discipline goal you can complete even when motivation is low.

- Remove one distraction that keeps you from showing up consistently.

- Ask God for the strength to stay disciplined even when progress feels invisible.

Quiet Prayer: Lord, thank You for being by my side even when my motivation fades. Help me choose discipline when emotions waver and effort feels unnoticed. Strengthen my commitment to honor You through consistency and obedience. Teach me to trust that You are working even when results come slowly. **Amen.**

JOURNALING & NOTES

8

TRAINING THE MIND DURING RECOVERY

"Do not conform to the pattern of this world, but be transformed
by the renewing of your mind."
Romans 12:2

Scripture Insight: Romans 12:2 reminds believers that real transformation begins in the mind. This verse challenges us to resist patterns shaped by pressure, comparison, doubt, and fear. Renewal happens when thinking aligns with God's truth rather than external expectations. A renewed mind leads to steady obedience even when circumstances feel limiting.

Recovery often exposes mental strain before physical weakness. Athletes may feel pressured to rush progress, compare timelines, or define worth by productivity. This Scripture calls injured athletes to guard their thoughts during recovery. God renews the mind when we choose truth over anxiety and patience over urgency. Healing involves mental discipline as much as physical care.

TESTED ON THE SIDELINES

Athlete Spotlight: Katie Ledecky is known for relentless consistency and mental toughness in distance swimming. During periods of illness and physical fatigue earlier in her career, she was forced to step back from full training and competition. Time away from peak performance disrupted routines that had long defined her success.

For an athlete built on repetition and endurance, recovery felt unsettling. Reduced training volume and altered schedules tested Katie's patience. Without daily validation from racing, mental focus became as important as physical conditioning. Staying disciplined in thought required intention.

Ledecky used these seasons to strengthen mental habits. Visualization, controlled routines, and focus on daily preparation replaced external results. Instead of allowing frustration to dominate, she committed to renewing her mindset during recovery. Her faith helped her remain grounded and disciplined in prayer when momentum slowed.

That mental training carried forward. By refusing to let uncertainty or comparison dictate her thoughts, Ledecky returned to swimming with clarity and confidence. Recovery became a place where discipline of the mind supported long-term excellence. Her example reflects the truth of Romans 12. Renewal begins internally before it shows externally. Athletes have to heal mentally before they heal on the outside.

CHAMPION YOUR FAITH

Personal Reflection: Recovery often slows the body but leaves the mind racing. Thoughts can drift toward comparison, fear, or impatience. Training the mind during recovery requires strict intention and discipline. Like Katie, you may be learning that progress begins with how you think. God invites you to renew your mind daily, even when physical limits remain. Healing includes learning to focus on truth rather than pressure and faith rather than frustration.

Reflection Questions: *What thoughts surface most often during recovery right now? Where am I tempted to compare my progress to others? How do my thoughts influence my patience and trust? What truth from God's Word can help renew my mindset today?*

Faith in Action:

- Identify one unhelpful thought pattern that is delaying your mental healing. Replace it with Scripture from Romans 12:2.

- Spend five quiet minutes practicing focused breathing and prayer to calm your mind.

- Limit exposure to content that fuels comparison or frustration during recovery.

- Thank God for one way He is strengthening your mind during this season.

Quiet Prayer: Father, thank You for caring about my mind as much as my body. Help me renew my thoughts with truth and patience as I recover. Guard me from fear and comparison, and strengthen my focus on You. Teach me to trust You as You restore both my body and my mindset. **Amen.**

JOURNALING & NOTES

9

SHOWING UP ON HARD DAYS

"Let us not become weary in doing good, for at the proper time we will reap a harvest if we do not give up."
Galatians 6:9

Scripture Insight: Galatians 6:9 speaks to perseverance when effort feels exhausting and results feel delayed. This verse tells us that weariness is real. It does not deny the feelings of fatigue or frustration. Instead, it encourages believers to keep showing up faithfully, trusting that God works beyond what is immediately visible.

Injury often makes doing good feel repetitive and unrewarding. Rehabilitation exercises, rest, and mental discipline can feel monotonous. Progress may be slow or inconsistent. This Scripture reminds injured athletes that faithfulness and mental strength still matters on hard days. God sees steady obedience, even when motivation fades and improvement feels small. The harvest comes in God's timing, not ours.

TESTED ON THE SIDELINES

Athlete Spotlight: Ben Zobrist faced seasons where showing up required more than physical strength. A shoulder injury and physical wear accumulated over years of professional baseball, affecting his consistency on the field and availability. Playing through pain and managing recovery became part of his daily life rather than an exception.

For a versatile player relied on in multiple roles, physical limitations tested his endurance. Some days required preparation without the guarantee of playing time or immediate payoff. Hard days blended together, marked by treatment, conditioning, and waiting rather than competition.

Zobrist chose to remain disciplined and present through those seasons. He continued preparing, supporting teammates, and honoring commitments even when his role felt uncertain. Faith anchored his perseverance. Showing up became an act of obedience rather than enthusiasm.

Those seasons reinforced a deeper truth. Faithfulness on difficult days builds character that lasts beyond performance. Zobrist's example reflects Galatians 6:9. Consistent effort, even when unseen or unrewarded, is not wasted. God brings growth and purpose in His timing.

CHAMPION YOUR FAITH

Personal Reflection: Hard days can drain energy and confidence. You may feel tired of repeating the same recovery work day in and day out, and wonder if the effort still matters. Showing up does not always feel heroic. Often it feels ordinary and exhausting. Like Ben, you may be learning that faithfulness is proven when you continue doing what is right even when motivation is gone. God honors consistency, especially on days that feel heavy and discouraging.

Reflection Questions: *What makes showing up feel hardest for me right now? Where do I feel weary or discouraged in recovery or training? What helps me stay faithful when motivation fades? How can I trust God's timing instead of measuring progress daily?*

Faith in Action:

- Identify one small rehab responsibility you can commit to today even if energy feels low.

- Complete today's recovery or preparation task without focusing on immediate results.

- Encourage someone else who may also be struggling to stay consistent in their recovery routine.

- Thank God for the strength to keep going even on difficult days.

Quiet Prayer: Gracious God, thank You for giving me strength to show up even when I feel tired or discouraged. Help me remain faithful when progress isn't quick and effort feels unnoticed. Renew my perseverance and remind me that You are working beyond what I can see. Teach me to trust Your timing and not give up. **Amen.**

JOURNALING & NOTES

10

GRIT WITHOUT THE SPOTLIGHT

"Whatever you do, work at it with all your heart, as working for the Lord, not for human masters."
Colossians 3:23

Scripture Insight: Colossians 3:23 redirects motivation from external recognition to internal faithfulness. This verse reminds believers that effort matters even when no one is watching. Working wholeheartedly for the Lord gives meaning to tasks that feel unseen or uncelebrated. Obedience is not dependent on applause.

Injury often removes visibility from an athlete's life. Recovery work takes place in quiet rooms. Progress goes unnoticed by teammates and coaches. This Scripture reminds injured athletes that effort still counts when the spotlight disappears. God sees work done in faith, even when recognition is absent. Faithfulness remains valuable because the purpose extends beyond public success.

TESTED ON THE SIDELINES

Athlete Spotlight: David Robinson of the San Antonio Spurs experienced a defining setback in 1996-1997 when back and foot injuries forced him into extended recovery. Surgery and rehabilitation limited his availability and reduced his role on the court.

For a player known for leadership and influence, being sidelined challenged his identity and pride.

Recovery required humility. Robinson could no longer contribute in the same visible ways. His training focused on rehabilitation rather than performance. Many of his hardest days involved quiet discipline without public acknowledgment or immediate results.

Instead of withdrawing, Robinson leaned into service and preparation. He remained committed to conditioning, mentoring teammates, and honoring responsibilities even when minutes and recognition were limited. His faith helped him reframe effort as service to God rather than pursuit of attention.

That season highlighted a deeper strength. Grit did not disappear when the spotlight faded. It matured. Robinson's willingness to work faithfully without recognition reflected the heart of Colossians 3:23. Robinson's purpose remained strong because his effort was rooted in obedience, not applause.

CHAMPION YOUR FAITH

Personal Reflection: Being injured can make effort feel invisible. You may wonder whether your work still matters when others receive the attention and opportunity. Grit without recognition requires a shift in motivation. You may be learning that faithfulness does not depend on praise. God values work done with integrity, even when no one notices. Purpose does not disappear when the spotlight fades.

Reflection Questions: *Where do I feel unseen or overlooked right now? How does lack of recognition affect my motivation? What helps me stay committed when effort feels unnoticed? How can I shift my focus from approval to obedience?*

Faith in Action:

- Choose one recovery exercise to complete today with full effort, regardless of recognition.

- Serve a teammate, coach, or family member without expecting acknowledgment.

- Remind yourself that God sees faithful work and mental grit even when others do not.

- Thank God for an opportunity to grow in humility and perseverance.

Quiet Prayer: Lord, thank You for seeing my efforts even when others do not. Help me work with integrity and purpose when recognition is absent. Strengthen my commitment to honor You through faithfulness and service. Teach me to find meaning in obedience rather than attention. **Amen.**

JOURNALING & NOTES

CHAPTER 3: RESILIENCE & RECOVERY

Getting Back Up Again and Again

11

BOUNCING BACK AFTER SETBACKS

"Though I have fallen, I will rise. Though I sit in darkness, the Lord will be my light."
Micah 7:8

Scripture Insight: Micah 7:8 speaks to resilience rooted in faith rather than circumstance. This verse directly and honestly acknowledges failure, pain, and darkness in difficult times. Falling is real. Sitting in darkness happens. Yet the declaration does not end there. Hope is anchored in the Lord, not in the absence of setbacks.

For athletes dealing with an injury, setbacks can feel final. Progress stalls. Confidence drops. Fear grows when recovery does not follow expectations. Micah reminds us that falling does not cancel God's work. Rising is possible because God remains present even in dark seasons. Faith does not erase the setback. It provides light and strength to stand again and rise above the darkness.

TESTED ON THE SIDELINES

Athlete Spotlight: Alex Smith experienced one of the most severe setbacks in professional football when he suffered a catastrophic leg injury during his 2018 season with the Washington Redskins. Multiple surgeries followed, and a life-threatening infection almost cost him his life and leg. The road ahead for Alex was a long and uncertain recovery. Doctors questioned whether he would walk normally again, let alone return to the field.

The injury forced Smith into 18 months of rehabilitation marked by intense pain, depression, and many setbacks. Progress came slowly and was often interrupted. Simple movements required patience and persistence. The darkness of uncertainty tested his resolve and emotional strength.

Instead of giving in to despair, Smith focused on incremental progress and faith. He committed to rehabilitation one day at a time, trusting that recovery was possible even when outcomes were unclear. His mindset shifted from immediate results to steady perseverance.

Smith's return to professional football was not defined by speed or spectacle. It was defined by resilience. His story reflects Micah's words. Falling did not end his purpose. God provided light through persistence, support, and faith. Alex's rising came through endurance shaped in the hardest moments.

CHAMPION YOUR FAITH

Personal Reflection: Setbacks can feel discouraging and exhausting. You may feel frustrated when recovery includes unexpected delays or repeated obstacles. Falling does not mean you have failed. It means you are facing resistance. Like Alex, you may be learning that rising often begins quietly through consistency and trust. God remains present in the dark moments, offering strength to keep moving forward even when progress feels slow.

Reflection Questions: *What setback has been most difficult for me to accept? Where do I feel discouraged or fearful right now? What helps me keep going when progress feels uncertain? How can I trust God to provide light during this season?*

Faith in Action:

- Identify one small sign of progress you may have overlooked and acknowledge it today.

- Commit to one recovery step today without dwelling on past setbacks.

- Speak encouragement to yourself when frustration rises.

- Thank God for the mental strength to rise again, even when the path feels extremely difficult.

Quiet Prayer: Heavenly Father, thank You for being my light when setbacks feel overwhelming. Help me rise up with courage and patience when results take time to appear. Strengthen my faith in you and remind me that setbacks do not define my future. Guide me forward with hope and trust in You. **Amen.**

JOURNALING & NOTES

12

WHEN PROGRESS FEELS SLOW

"Let perseverance finish its work so that you may be mature and complete, not lacking anything."
James 1:4

Scripture Insight: Isaiah James 1:4 emphasizes the importance of allowing perseverance to do its full work. This verse does not promise quick improvement or immediate relief. It calls believers to remain steady through difficulty so growth can reach completion. Maturity develops through endurance, not speed.

For athletes, slow progress can feel discouraging and unfair. Recovery may move in small increments that feel insignificant day to day. Physical setbacks can interrupt momentum and test patience. This Scripture reminds us that perseverance has purpose even when progress feels invisible. God uses sustained effort and trust over time to build mental toughness that lasts beyond physical recovery. Internal healing and growth continue even when improvement feels delayed.

TESTED ON THE SIDELINES

Athlete Spotlight: Klay Thompson, a NBA shooting guard for the Golden State Warriors, faced an extended recovery after suffering two major injuries in consecutive seasons. A torn ACL was followed by an Achilles injury, forcing him into nearly two full years away from competition. The long absence challenged his rhythm, his identity, confidence, and patience.

Rehabilitation was slow and demanding. Progress came in slow stages rather than breakthroughs. Simple movements required repetition and restraint. Watching teammates compete while he remained on the bench tested his resolve and emotional endurance on a daily basis.

Instead of rushing recovery, Thompson committed to perseverance and patience. He trusted the process of rehabilitation even when improvement felt minimal. Day by day, he focused on conditioning, strength, and mental readiness. Allowing perseverance to finish its work required intentional discipline and humility.

That season reshaped Thompson's approach to progress. Returning to competition took time and patience, but perseverance carried him forward. His experience reflects James 1:4. Growth and readiness were built through endurance, not shortcuts. Completion came through steady commitment rather than speed.

CHAMPION YOUR FAITH

Personal Reflection: Slow progress can challenge your confidence and outlook. You may feel tempted to rush healing or question whether effort still matters. Perseverance asks you to stay committed when results are delayed. Like Klay, you may be learning that endurance produces growth that quick fixes cannot. God works through consistent effort, shaping your work ethic and resolve even when progress feels minimal. Trusting this process requires patience and faith.

Reflection Questions: *Where do I feel most impatient with my recovery right now? How does slow progress affect my motivation and outlook? What helps me stay committed when improvement feels small? How can I allow perseverance to finish its work in me?*

Faith in Action:

- Identify one area where progress feels slow and commit to staying intentionally patient today.

- Complete your recovery or training task without rushing the outcome.

- Encourage yourself by recognizing one small improvement you have noticed this week.

- Thank God for building endurance and maturity through this season.

Quiet Prayer: Lord my God, thank You for working through me even when progress feels minimal. Help me remain patient and committed as perseverance does its work within me. Strengthen my trust in You when improvement feels delayed. Teach me to rely on work ethic and endurance and rather than speed. **Amen.**

JOURNALING & NOTES

13

STRENGTH BUILT IN SILENCE

"For no one is cast off by the Lord forever. Though He brings grief, He will show compassion, so great is His unfailing love."
Lamentations 3:31–32

Scripture Insight: Lamentations 3:31–32 speaks hope into seasons marked by loss and quiet suffering. These verses acknowledge grief without minimizing it. Pain is real. Loss is heavy. Yet God's compassion is promised alongside sorrow. Being brought low does not mean being abandoned.

Injury often creates silence around an athlete. Applause fades. Attention shifts. Recovery happens away from teammates, crowds, and competition. This Scripture reminds us that God's compassion is not withdrawn in quiet seasons. Even when progress feels unseen and disappointment feels personal, God remains attentive and loving. Strength is often formed in moments where no one else is watching.

TESTED ON THE SIDELINES

Athlete Spotlight: During the 2009-2020 seasons, **Kerri Walsh Jennings** dealt with recurrent shoulder problems, especially related to the rotator cuff and labrum, which are common in elite volleyball players due to repetitive overhead motion. Time away from competition forced her into extended rehabilitation and limited visibility. For an athlete accustomed to intensity and momentum, the silence of recovery felt devastating.

Kerri's rehabilitation required patience and restraint. Progress came slowly through repetitive work and careful conditioning. Without competition or crowds, motivation had to come from internal discipline and faith rather than excitement. The quiet days tested her mental endurance more than the matches ever had.

Instead of internally withdrawing, Walsh Jennings leaned into faith during these silent seasons. She trusted that growth was still happening even when results were not visible. Recovery became a place where resilience and humility were refined. Her strength developed quietly through consistency and trust.

Those seasons did not diminish Kerri's impact. They deepened it. By allowing strength to form in silence, she returned with grit and purpose. Her experience reflects Lamentations 3. Grief may come, but compassion follows. God remains present, shaping strength even in the quiet.

CHAMPION YOUR FAITH

Personal Reflection: Silence can feel uncomfortable and isolating. Injury may remove recognition and replace it with quiet routines and long days of recovery. Strength built in silence often goes unnoticed at first. Like Kerri, you may be learning that God works deeply in these moments. Growth does not always announce it-self. Your faith and mindset is strengthened when you continue trusting God without affirmation or attention.

Reflection Questions: *Where does silence feel most difficult for me right now? What emotions surface when recognition is removed? How can I trust that God is still working when progress feels unseen? What kind of strength might God be building quietly in me?*

Faith in Action:

- Spend ten quiet minutes in prayer or reflection without distractions today.

- Commit to completing your recovery routine today with focus and patience.

- Resist the urge to measure progress by recognition or comparison.

- Thank God for working in unseen ways during this season.

Quiet Prayer: Thank You, God, for being close to me even in silence. Help me trust Your compassion when progress feels hidden and attention fades. Strengthen my resilience as You work quietly within me. Teach me to remain faithful and patient in this season. **Amen.**

JOURNALING & NOTES

14

REFUSING TO QUIT

"We are hard pressed on every side, but not crushed; perplexed, but not in despair; persecuted, but not abandoned; struck down, but not destroyed."
2 Corinthians 4:8–9

Scripture Insight: 2 Corinthians 4:8–9 acknowledges pressure, confusion, and pain without pretending they do not exist. This verse lists real struggles that press believers from every side, yet pairs each one with a truth that limits its power. Experiencing a hardship does not mean being destroyed. God allows hardship, but He does not abandon His people within it.

Injury often creates this exact tension for athletes. You may feel overwhelmed, uncertain, and knocked down by setbacks, yet still able to move forward. This Scripture reminds us that endurance is possible even when circumstances feel heavy. When you refuse to quit, you are not relying on your own strength alone. You are standing on the truth that God sustains you, even when the road feels difficult.

TESTED ON THE SIDELINES

Athlete Spotlight: Jeremy Lin's career was marked by repeated setbacks that tested perseverance. After his 'Linsanity" break-through moments on the New York Knicks, injuries and roster changes disrupted his continuity. Knee and hamstring issues limited playing time and forced extended recovery, often just as momentum seemed to build. Each setback raised questions about his durability and future opportunity.

For a guard whose game relied on speed, agility, and confidence, injury created both physical and mental strain. Time away from the court meant watching opportunities pass him by while uncertainty about his future grew. Rehabilitation required perseverance and patience without guarantees. The pressure to return quickly competed with the need to heal fully.

Instead of quitting and giving up, Lin chose persistence. He continued preparing, rehabbing, and staying ready even when contracts and minutes on the court were uncertain. Faith grounded his resolve. Refusing to quit became a daily decision shaped by mental discipline rather than headlines or validation.

Those seasons revealed resilience forged under pressure. Lin's willingness to endure reflected the truth of the Scripture. Being struck down did not destroy his purpose or identity. By continuing forward through setbacks, he demonstrated strength sustained by faith, even when circumstances felt stacked against him.

CHAMPION YOUR FAITH

Personal Reflection: Setbacks in your recovery can make quitting feel reasonable. Injury, repeated delays, and uncertainty can drain your confidence. Refusing to quit does not mean ignoring pain or forcing progress. It means choosing faithfulness and patience when pressure builds and answers are limited. Similar to Jeremy, you may be learning that perseverance is built through steady commitment rather than dramatic breakthroughs. God's strength sustains you even when improvement is not obvious and the road feels heavy.

Reflection Questions: *Where do I feel most tempted to give up right now? What pressures make perseverance feel difficult? How do setbacks affect my confidence and trust? What helps me keep going when results take longer to appear?*

Faith in Action:

- Identify one area in your recovery where quitting feels tempting and commit to staying faithful today.

- Complete one recovery step or training rep without focusing on outcomes.

- Replace a discouraging thought with a truth from 2 Corinthians 4:8–9.

- Thank God for His presence in seasons that feel difficult to carry.

Quiet Prayer: Father, thank You for sustaining me when pressure feels overwhelming. Help me refuse to quit when setbacks test my resolve. Strengthen my faith as I heal and remind me that I am not abandoned in this season. Teach me to endure with courage and trust. **Amen.**

JOURNALING & NOTES

15

RISING FROM DISAPPOINTMENT

"The righteous person may have many troubles, but the Lord delivers him from them all."
Psalm 34:19

Scripture Insight: Psalm 34:19 speaks honestly about hardship. It does not suggest that faith prevents trouble or removes disappointment. Instead, it acknowledges that righteous people still face many challenges. The promise is not the absence of pain, but the presence and deliverance of the Lord through it.

To athletes, disappointment often feels layered. Setbacks interrupt progress. Expectations fall short. Hope can feel shattered when recovery does not unfold as planned. This Scripture reminds us that trouble is not evidence of failure or abandonment. God's deliverance may not come instantly, but it is certain. Faith rests not in avoiding disappointment, but in trusting that God remains active, faithful, and present through every trial.

TESTED ON THE SIDELINES

Athlete Spotlight: J.J. Watt faced repeated injury setbacks during the prime of his career on the Houston Texans. Major surgeries and long recovery periods followed seasons cut short by physical breakdown. Each injury brought more disappointment, not only because of missed games, but because expectations for impact and leadership were disrupted.

For a player known for intensity and preparation, being sidelined was emotionally difficult for Watt. Rehabilitation demanded resilience and restraint rather than action. Watching teammates compete while he worked through recovery tested his resolve and confidence.

Instead of withdrawing, Watt committed fully to rehabilitation, training, and preparation. He approached recovery with strict discipline, refusing to let disappointment define his response. Faith and purpose helped him reframe setbacks as challenges to overcome rather than reasons to quit.

Those seasons reshaped his resilience. Rising from disappointment required humility, patience, and trust. Watt's resilience reflects the truth of Psalm 34. Trouble may come, but it does not have the final word. God remains faithful to deliver, strengthen, and restore through endurance and faith.

CHAMPION YOUR FAITH

Personal Reflection: Disappointment can feel heavy and discouraging. You may feel frustrated by missed opportunities or delayed recovery. Rising from disappointment does not mean ignoring how you feel. It means choosing faith when expectations fall apart. Like J.J., you may be learning that resilience grows when disappointment is met with resilience rather than defeat. God remains faithful even when outcomes differ from what you hoped.

Reflection Questions: *What disappointment feels hardest for me to process right now in this moment? How has this injury affected my confidence or hope? What helps me move forward when expectations fall short? How can I trust God's deliverance even when change comes gradually?*

Faith in Action:

- Acknowledge one disappointment that is weighing on you and bring it to God in prayer today.

- Focus on your recovery, training and preparation tasks with renewed hope.

- Encourage yourself by recalling a past situation where perseverance paid off.

- Thank God for His presence even when outcomes differ from expectations.

Quiet Prayer: My Lord, thank You for being with me in this season, even when I feel overlooked and broken down. Help me trust that Your calling and purpose for me have not changed because my circumstances have. Give me patience as I heal and confidence that I am still chosen by You. **Amen.**

JOURNALING & NOTES

CHAPTER 4: PATIENCE & PERSEVERANCE

Staying Faithful Through The Long Season

16

ONE DAY AT A TIME

"Therefore do not worry about tomorrow, for tomorrow will worry about itself. Each day has enough trouble of its own."
Matthew 6:34

Scripture Insight: Matthew 6:34 speaks directly to anxiety about the future. Jesus does not deny that trouble exists. He acknowledges it plainly. What He challenges is the habit of carrying tomorrow's weight today. Worry multiplies pressure and drains mental strength that is meant for the present moment.

Injury often pulls athletes into the future too quickly. Questions about timelines, return dates, and performance can overwhelm the mind. This Scripture reminds us that God gives grace one day at a time. Healing is not meant to be rushed mentally or physically. Trust grows when focus stays on what God is doing today rather than fearing what may or may not happen tomorrow.

TESTED ON THE SIDELINES

Athlete Spotlight: Outfielder for the Phillie's, **Bryce Harper**'s season changed suddenly when a serious elbow injury required surgery and altered his expectations. Instead of building momentum on the field, he faced a long recovery filled with uncertainty about strength, timing, and his long-term impact on the field.

Rehabilitation demanded patience. Progress came in controlled stages, not bursts of achievement. Daily routines replaced game-day adrenaline. Focusing too far ahead only added frustration for Bryce. The future felt heavy when outcomes remained unclear.

Harper adjusted by narrowing his focus. Recovery became about showing up each day and completing the work in front of him. Rather than rushing milestones, he committed to the discipline of daily progress. Faith helped anchor his mindset when the unknowns threatened to dominate his thoughts.

That approach allowed healing to unfold steadily. Taking recovery one day at a time protected both his body and mind. Harper's experience reflects the wisdom of Jesus' words. Peace grows when attention stays rooted in today, trusting that tomorrow will be handled by God in his own timing.

CHAMPION YOUR FAITH

Personal Reflection: Injury can make the future feel intimidating. You may find your thoughts racing ahead to outcomes you cannot control. Living one day at a time does not mean lowering your expectations. It means placing trust where it belongs. Just like Bryce, you may be learning that healing happens best when focus stays on today's responsibilities rather than tomorrow's worries. God provides internal strength for the present moment, not the entire future at once.

Reflection Questions: *What future worry weighs most heavily on my mind right now? How does focusing too far ahead affect my peace and patience? How can I fully commit to today's recovery plan or rest day? How can I trust God with tomorrow instead of carrying it myself?*

Faith in Action:

- Write down one future concern and intentionally set it aside for today.

- Show up fully for today's work, even if it feels monotonous.

- Practice redirecting anxious thoughts back to the present moment.

- Thank God for the grace and strength He provides for today.

Quiet Prayer: Dear God, thank You for meeting me in this moment and not asking me to carry tomorrow's weight. Help me focus on today with perseverance and patience as I heal. Calm my anxious thoughts and remind me that You are already present in what lies ahead. Teach me to walk forward one day at a time. **Amen.**

JOURNALING & NOTES

17

FAITHFUL IN PHYSICAL THERAPY

"Whoever can be trusted with very little can also be trusted with much, and whoever is dishonest with very little will also be dishonest with much."
Luke 16:10

Scripture Insight: Luke 16:10 teaches that faithfulness is proven in small responsibilities before larger ones are given. Jesus emphasizes that trust is built through consistency, not significance. What feels minor or unnoticed still matters deeply to God. Faithfulness is measured by obedience, not visibility.

For injured athletes, physical therapy can feel insignificant compared to competition. Repetitive movements, slow progress, and quiet sessions often feel disconnected from bigger goals. This Scripture reminds us that God values faithfulness in these small steps. Showing up fully to recovery work reflects trustworthiness. When an athlete honors the small tasks, God uses them to prepare the heart and body for greater responsibility ahead.

TESTED ON THE SIDELINES

Athlete Spotlight: Long before returning to dominance as a NFL defensive end, **Reggie White** spent several seasons working through injuries that demanded discipline away from the spotlight. Over the course of his long career, White played through chronic back, knee, and shoulder pain, enduring the physical toll of constant double teams and the demands of football season after season. Physical wear and repeated strain required focused rehabilitation and conditioning. For a player known for power and impact, progress often depended on patient, repetitive recovery work.

Physical therapy tested White's humility. The work was quiet and methodical. There were no crowds, no recognition, and no immediate payoff. Strength had to be rebuilt through perseverance rather than force. Each session required commitment to details that felt small compared to game-day moments.

White approached recovery with seriousness and faith. He showed up prepared, worked through routines, and respected the process even when results were gradual. He treated physical therapy as a responsibility to steward rather than an obstacle to rush through. That faithfulness paid dividends. By honoring small steps, White rebuilt his strength and longevity. His experience reflects Luke's teaching. Trust is formed through consistency in the unseen work. Being faithful in little things prepared him for a greater impact when the opportunity returned.

CHAMPION YOUR FAITH

Personal Reflection: Physical therapy can feel repetitive and discouraging. You may wonder how small movements and slow progress connect to bigger goals. Faithfulness in this season is not about excitement. It is about responsibility. Like Reggie, you may be learning that discipline in quiet spaces matters deeply. God uses consistency in small tasks to shape trust, patience, and readiness for what comes next.

Reflection Questions: *What part of physical therapy feels hardest to stay committed to right now? Where am I tempted to rush through my therapy instead of honoring the process? How do small daily choices reflect my trust in God? What would faithful obedience look like for me today?*

Faith in Action:

- Commit to completing today's physical therapy exercises with focus and patience.

- Treat one small recovery task as an act of worship rather than obligation.

- Resist comparing your progress to others and stay attentive to your own process.

- Thank God for the opportunity to grow through patience and perseverance.

Quiet Prayer: Lord, thank You for teaching me the value of faithfulness in small things. Help me honor the recovery work in front of me with patience and integrity. Strengthen my trust as I commit to each step of healing. Prepare me for what lies ahead as I remain faithful today. **Amen.**

JOURNALING & NOTES

18

ENDURANCE THROUGH PAIN

"Not only so, but we also glory in our sufferings, because we know that suffering produces perseverance; perseverance, character; and character, hope.
Romans 5:3–4

Scripture Insight: Romans 5:3–4 presents a progression that challenges how we view pain. Suffering is not described as meaningless or wasted. It is the starting point for perseverance, which shapes character and leads to hope. This Scripture does not celebrate pain itself. It reveals how God uses hardship to build strength that lasts.

For injured athletes, pain often feels like an interruption rather than a teacher. Physical discomfort, limitations, and setbacks can drain confidence and patience. This passage reminds us that endurance grows through sustained effort in difficult conditions. When an athlete continues forward despite pain, God uses that perseverance to shape character. Hope follows not because pain disappears, but because faith is strengthened through it.

TESTED ON THE SIDELINES

Athlete Spotlight: Bethany Hamilton is a professional surfer whose career was forever changed in 2003 when she lost her left arm in a shark attack while surfing off the coast of Hawaii. The injury required emergency surgery, extensive rehabilitation, and a complete relearning of balance and strength before she could return to competitive surfing. Endurance was no longer optional; pain management, adaptation, and persistence became part of everyday life on her path back to the water.

Surfing demanded physical balance, strength, and confidence, all of which had to be rebuilt. Training sessions required adaptation and patience. Enduring pain was not about ignoring it. It meant learning how to work through limitations safely and consistently. Progress came through perseverance rather than speed.

Hamilton relied on faith and gratitude to endure. She focused on what she could do rather than what had been lost. Perseverance became a daily commitment rooted in trust rather than circumstance. Pain did not define her future. It shaped her resilience and purpose.

Her story reflects Romans 5. Suffering produced perseverance. Perseverance shaped character. Character gave rise to hope. Perseverance through pain did not weaken her faith. It strengthened it and carried her forward with confidence and courage.

CHAMPION YOUR FAITH

Personal Reflection: Pain can wear down both body and spirit. You may feel tired of pushing through discomfort or discouraged by limitations. Endurance is not about denying pain. It is about continuing forward with faith when pain is present. You may be learning that perseverance builds strength you cannot gain any other way. God uses endurance to shape character and renew hope, even when recovery feels demanding.

Reflection Questions: *Where am I struggling most with pain right now? How does pain affect my patience and attitude? What helps me keep going when discomfort persists? How can I trust God to build hope through perseverance?*

Faith in Action:

- Acknowledge one area of pain honestly and ask God for strength to endure it today.

- Complete your physical therapy today with focus rather than frustration.

- Adjust expectations to protect healing while remaining faithful to effort.

- Thank God for the perseverance He is building within you through this season.

Quiet Prayer: Heavenly Father, thank You for strengthening me when pain feels heavy and progress feels demanding. Help me endure with patience and trust as You shape my character. Renew my hope as I continue healing and moving forward. Teach me to rely on You through every step of endurance. **Amen.**

JOURNALING & NOTES

19

OBEDIENCE IN THE SMALL STEPS

"Do not despise these small beginnings, for the Lord rejoices to see the work begin."
Zechariah 4:10

Scripture Insight: Zechariah 4:10 addresses discouragement that comes when progress looks unimpressive. God reminds us that beginnings matter, even when they feel small or slow. What appears insignificant to us is not overlooked by Him. Faithfulness at the start is worthy of joy in God's eyes.

For injured athletes, recovery often begins with steps that feel far removed from competition. Early movements can feel tedious and disconnected from long-term goals. This Scripture reminds us that obedience in small steps is not wasted effort. God values consistency in the early stages of healing. When an athlete honors the process without despising the beginning, God uses those moments to build strength, trust, and readiness for what comes next.

TESTED ON THE SIDELINES

Athlete Spotlight: After a major Achilles injury, **Kirk Cousins** of the Minnesota Vikings entered a recovery season defined by slow healing and progress. The injury disrupted his routine and raised questions about the timing and readiness of his return to the football field. Early rehabilitation focused on controlled movements and gradual progress rather than visible milestones.

For a quarterback used to preparation and structure, the small steps tested his discipline. Progress was measured in stability, balance, and repetition rather than performance. Each session required focus on small details that felt distant from game-day demands.

Cousins approached recovery with consistency and accountability. He committed to rehabilitation tasks fully, even when progress felt slow. Faith and patience helped him stay grounded in the process rather than frustrated by pace. Obedience in the daily work became a priority.

That commitment significantly shaped his recovery. By honoring small beginnings, Cousins rebuilt his strength methodically. His experience reflects Zechariah's message. God rejoices in faithful steps taken early. Obedience in small moments prepares athletes for greater responsibility when the opportunity returns.

CHAMPION YOUR FAITH

Personal Reflection: Small steps can feel discouraging when you want visible progress. Early recovery work may seem far disconnected from your long-term goals. Obedience in this season requires trust. You may be learning that consistency matters more than speed. God does not ask you to skip ahead. He asks you to be faithful where you are. Growth begins when you honor the work in front of you.

Reflection Questions: *What small step feels hardest to value right now? Where am I tempted to rush my recovery instead of trusting the process? How do small acts of obedience reflect my faith? How can I fully commit to today's work?*

Faith in Action:

- Identify one small recovery task that seems unimportant and complete it with focus and care.

- Resist the urge to measure progress against future milestones.

- Speak gratitude for the ability to begin, even if it is small steps of progress.

- Thank God for rejoicing in faithful obedience, no matter how small it feels.

Quiet Prayer: My Lord and God, thank You for valuing faithfulness in small beginnings. Help me honor each step of recovery with patience and trust. Strengthen my commitment to obedience when progress feels slow. Teach me to trust that You are working through every small act of faith. **Amen.**

JOURNALING & NOTES

20

TRUSTING THE PROCESS

*"The Lord makes firm the steps of the one who delights in Him;
though he may stumble, he will not fall, for the Lord upholds him
with His hand."*
Psalm 37:23–24

Scripture Insight: Psalm 37:23–24 speaks to steady progress guided by God rather than quick results driven by pressure. These verses acknowledge that stumbles happen along the way. Trust is not defined by perfection. It is defined by God's steady presence and support through each step.

Many times the recovery process can feel uncertain and uneven. Some days bring progress, while others bring frustration or setbacks. This Scripture reminds us that God is involved in every step, not just the finish line. Even when progress feels slow or uneven, God remains actively guiding and sustaining. Trusting the process means believing that God is working through each phase of healing, even when results are not immediate.

TESTED ON THE SIDELINES

Athlete Spotlight: Alex Morgan is a U.S. Women's National Team forward and World Cup champion who faced disrupted seasons after a knee injury in 2017 that limited her availability and rhythm during club and international play. Time away from full competition forced her to slow down, manage recovery carefully, and resist the urge to rush back before her body was ready. Returning to form required patience, discipline, and trust in a process that could not be accelerated.

For a soccer forward used to constant movement and intensity, rehabilitation tested Alex's restraint. Training plans shifted. Progress came in phases rather than breakthroughs. Each step forward required trust that the process itself mattered, even when her momentum felt slow.

Morgan approached recovery with discipline and focus. She committed to every step of conditioning, rehabilitation, and gradual return without forcing outcomes. Faith helped her remain grounded when progress did not follow expectations. Trust became less about speed and more about consistency.

That commitment allowed healing to unfold steadily. By trusting the process rather than fighting it, Morgan returned to soccer prepared and resilient. Her experience reflects the promise of Psalm 37. Even when steps feel uncertain, God remains present, firming each one along the way.

CHAMPION YOUR FAITH

Personal Reflection: The recovery process can test your patience and perseverance. You may feel tempted to rush progress or question whether effort is paying off. Trusting the process requires faith in what you cannot yet see. Like Alex, you may be learning that consistency matters more than speed. God does not abandon you when progress feels slow. He is present in each step, strengthening and guiding you forward.

Reflection Questions: *Where do I feel impatient with my recovery right now? What makes trusting the process difficult for me? How do setbacks in my recovery challenge my confidence and identity? What helps me remain steady when progress feels uneven?*

Faith in Action:

- Identify one part of your recovery that requires a lot of patience from you.

- Complete today's stretching or rehabilitation routine without rushing the outcome.

- Replace frustration with prayer when progress feels slow.

- Thank God for guiding each step, even when results are not immediate.

Quiet Prayer: Dear God, thank You for guiding my steps and holding me steady through this recovery process. Help me trust You when my healing doesn't come quickly. Strengthen my patience and faith as I continue to heal. **Amen.**

JOURNALING & NOTES

CHAPTER 5: HOPE & HEALING

Believing God Still Has More

21

HOPE WHEN THE TIMELINE CHANGES

"For the revelation awaits an appointed time; it speaks of the end and will not prove false. Though it linger, wait for it; it will certainly come and will not delay."
Habakkuk 2:3

Scripture Insight: Habakkuk 2:3 addresses the tension between promise and timing. God makes it clear that fulfillment does not always happen quickly, but it will happen at the right time. Waiting does not mean the promise has failed. It means God's timing is still at work beyond what we can see.

When you have an injury, changing timelines can feel discouraging and unsettling. Return dates shift. Expectations must be adjusted. Progress that once felt predictable becomes uncertain. God's purpose for you remains intact even when schedules change. Waiting becomes an act of trust that God is faithful to complete the plan He has begun, even when patience is tested.

TESTED ON THE SIDELINES

Athlete Spotlight: Stacy Lewis is a professional golfer who competed at the highest level while managing chronic back pain caused by scoliosis, a condition that required major spinal surgery in 2010. Even after returning to competition, stiffness, fatigue, and physical limitations regularly disrupted her training and tournament rhythm. For a golfer accustomed to structure and preparation, changing timelines and waiting on delayed progress required mental and emotional flexibility.

Recovery demanded patience. Progress did not always align with planned return dates. Time away from competition tested her confidence and created uncertainty about her readiness. Each adjustment required letting go of expectations and trusting a slower pace.

Lewis approached these seasons with discipline and resolve. She focused on daily therapy and rehabilitation rather than fixed deadlines. Faith helped her remain steady when timelines shifted and outcomes felt unclear. Hope became rooted in persistence rather than schedules.

That patience and hope allowed her to return to competing with a greater purpose. By trusting God through changing timelines, Lewis demonstrated that hope does not disappear when plans change. Her experience reflects Habakkuk's promise. What God sets in motion will come to pass, even when the waiting stretches longer than expected.

CHAMPION YOUR FAITH

Personal Reflection: When recovery or progress does not follow the timeline you expected, frustration can quietly take over. Delays have a way of making effort feel wasted and goals feel farther away. Yet growth does not stop simply because the schedule changes. Similar to Stacy, you may be learning that hope is not built on perfect timing, but on steady trust when outcomes remain uncertain. Progress still happens in ways you may not see right away. Waiting does not mean you are falling behind. It means trust is being strengthened in a different way.

Reflection Questions: *How have changing timelines affected my hope or confidence? Where do I feel most frustrated by delays right now? What helps me remain hopeful when plans shift unexpectedly? How can I trust God's timing instead of my own schedule?*

Faith in Action:

- Identify one expectation about timing that drains your level of hope. Offer it up to God.

- Commit to the work in front of you instead of the timeline ahead.

- Practice patience by resisting the urge to compare timelines with others.

- Thank God for keeping you hopeful even when waiting feels long.

Quiet Prayer: Thank You, Lord, for reminding me that Your timing is trustworthy even when mine feels uncertain. Help me remain hopeful as I wait and adjust to changing plans. Strengthen my patience and faith when progress feels delayed. Teach me to trust that what You have promised will come in Your perfect timing. **Amen.**

JOURNALING & NOTES

22

LIGHT IN THE DARK SEASON

"Why, my soul, are you downcast? Why so disturbed within me? Put your hope in God, for I will yet praise Him, my Savior and my God."
Psalm 42:11

Scripture Insight: Psalm 42:11 captures an honest inner struggle. The writer speaks directly to his own soul, acknowledging discouragement instead of hiding it. This verse shows that faith does not ignore sadness or disappointment. It confronts them with truth. Hope is not found by denying pain, but by intentionally placing trust in God even when emotions feel heavy.

Injury can create a dark season for athletes. Isolation, uncertainty, and loss of purpose can leave the soul feeling downcast. This Scripture reminds us that feeling discouraged does not mean faith is failing. It means the soul needs direction. Choosing hope in God during darkness is an act of faith. Even when circumstances remain difficult, God offers light, strength, and promise to keep moving forward one day at a time.

TESTED ON THE SIDELINES

Athlete Spotlight: Kayla Harrison is a two-time Olympic gold medalist in judo who faced repeated physical setbacks, including a serious knee injury that required ACL surgery in 2018, just as she was transitioning into professional MMA. Extended rehabilitation, lingering pain, and the challenge of rebuilding strength put her into a dark season were she was forced to slow down and relearn trust in her body.

Recovery required more than physical strength. Pain, isolation, and emotional fatigue tested her resilience. Without immediate results or visibility, training demanded mental endurance and hope. The darkness of recovery moments forced doubts to surface .

Harrison leaned heavily on her faith during these seasons. She chose to confront discouragement honestly rather than ignore it. Discipline, prayer, and consistency became anchors when motivation felt distant. Hope was rebuilt slowly through trust rather than circumstances.

Those dark seasons did not define her limits. They revealed her strength. By choosing hope during discouragement, Harrison demonstrated that light can exist even when circumstances feel heavy. Her experience reflects Psalm 42. Hope placed in God sustains athletes through seasons where clarity and momentum are absent.

CHAMPION YOUR FAITH

Personal Reflection: Dark seasons can feel isolating and heavy. Injury may bring emotional weight that feels difficult to explain or escape. Choosing to have hope in these moments requires honesty and courage. To get through the dark days, you must choose trust when emotions feel overwhelming. God offers light even when the path ahead feels unclear.

Reflection Questions: *Where do I feel most discouraged right now? What emotions surface when recovery seems so far away? How do I usually respond when my mood feels heavy? What helps me place hope in God during dark seasons?*

Faith in Action:

- Acknowledge one discouraging emotion honestly in prayer today.

- Spend time in a quiet space to reflect on your emotions without distractions.

- Reach out to someone you trust instead of isolating yourself.

- Thank God for being present even when the dark days feel heavy.

Quiet Prayer: Thank You, Gracious Lord, for staying near to me when my soul feels downcast. Help me place my hope in You during this dark season. Lift my spirit as I heal and remind me that Your light has not faded. Strengthen my faith and give me hope when emotions feel heavy and progress is stalled. **Amen.**

JOURNALING & NOTES

23

GOD IS NOT FINISHED

"Being confident of this, that He who began a good work in you will carry it on to completion until the day of Christ Jesus."
Philippians 1:6

Scripture Insight: Philippians 1:6 reminds us that God finishes what He starts. Growth is not abandoned halfway through difficulty. Completion belongs to God's timing and faithfulness, not human strength or consistency.

As an athlete, you may question whether healing, confidence, or opportunity will fully return. This Scripture speaks directly to that fear. God's work does not stop because circumstances change. Delays, setbacks, and pauses do not cancel His purpose for you. When healing feels unfinished, faith rests in the truth that God continues working even when results are not yet visible.

TESTED ON THE SIDELINES

Athlete Spotlight: Peyton Manning suffered a serious neck injury in 2011 that required multiple surgeries, including a spinal fusion. The injury caused him to miss the entire 2011 NFL season with the Indianapolis Colts and put his career in doubt. Strength, timing, and control were uncertain. Many doubted whether he would return to professional play at all.

Rebuilding began with controlled movements and short, deliberate sessions rather than full throws. Each step forward required restraint, not urgency. Improvement came through steady repetition instead of quick reassurance, forcing trust in the work long before results were visible.

Manning committed fully to his physical therapy and rehab routines. He approached recovery with focus, preparation, and faith. Instead of rushing results, he trusted the process and honored each stage of healing. His confidence grew gradually as strength returned.

That season did not mark the end of his career. It revealed perseverance. By trusting that his story was not finished, Manning returned prepared and purposeful. His experience reflects Philippians 1:6. Even in hardship, God remains active, shaping growth long before results are clear.

CHAMPION YOUR FAITH

Personal Reflection: Injury can make the future feel unfinished and unclear. You may wonder whether healing, confidence, or opportunity will fully return. Feeling incomplete does not mean God has stopped working. God is not finished with you, even when progress feels incomplete. Trust grows when you believe that healing and your purpose are still unfolding.

Reflection Questions: *Where do I feel incomplete or uncertain right now? What fears surface when progress feels unfinished? How does trusting God's completion change my perspective? What helps me stay patient and hopeful when healing feels slow?*

Faith in Action:

- Identify one area where progress feels unfinished and place it intentionally in God's hands.

- Release the pressure of outcomes and focus on what is required today.

- Remind yourself that growth continues even when results are not immediate.

- Thank God for remaining faithful to complete His work in you.

Quiet Prayer: Thank You, God, for shaping me in ways I cannot yet see. Help me trust that You are not finished with my healing or purpose. Strengthen my patience as I move forward step by step. Remind me that You always complete what You begin. **Amen.**

JOURNALING & NOTES

24

EXPECTING GOOD AGAIN

"For I know the plans I have for you," declares the Lord, "plans to prosper you and not to harm you, plans to give you hope and a future."
Jeremiah 29:11

Scripture Insight: Jeremiah 29:11 speaks to hope rooted in God's faithfulness rather than current circumstances. This verse speaks to those living in disruption and uncertainty, not comfort.

Injury can make expecting good feel risky. Pain, setbacks, and disappointment can harden the heart against hope. This Scripture reminds injured athletes that God's plans are not erased by interruption. It means trusting that God's intentions remain steady even when recovery feels ta. Hope becomes possible when faith rests in who God is, not in how fast progress appears.

TESTED ON THE SIDELINES

Athlete Spotlight: Shaun White is a three-time Olympic gold medalist and one of the most influential snowboarders in history. Over the course of his career, he endured several serious injuries, including a major knee injury in 2008 that required surgery and threatened his ability to compete at the highest level. Later, in 2017, a violent training crash left him with facial fractures and required multiple surgeries, forcing an extended recovery and raising real questions about whether his body could withstand another Olympic run. Each setback demanded patience, resilience, and the willingness to rebuild confidence after time away from competition.

Recovery challenged both body and mindset. Fear of reinjury and uncertainty about performance tested Shaun's confidence. Expecting success again required trust, patience, and resilience. Progress came gradually through rehabilitation and careful preparation rather than bold risk.

White chose to believe that his best moments were not behind him. He committed to recovery, rebuilt strength, and returned to training with renewed focus. Expecting good again required courage after disappointment. Faith and determination helped him move forward rather than retreat.

Those seasons reshaped his resilience. By choosing hope after setbacks, White demonstrated that belief in the future can return even after pain. His experience reflects Jeremiah's promise. God's plans remain intact, offering hope and direction beyond injury and fear.

CHAMPION YOUR FAITH

Personal Reflection: Injury can make hope feel fragile. You may hesitate to expect good again after disappointment or pain. Trusting God with the future requires courage and intention. God's plans are not limited by injury or delay. Expecting good again begins with trusting His plan more than your fear.

Reflection Questions: *What makes it difficult for me to expect good in my recovery right now? How has injury affected my confidence in the future? What fears hold me back from hoping again? How can I place my trust in God's plans rather than past disappointment?*

Faith in Action:

- Identify one fear that keeps you from expecting a good outcome and surrender it to God today.

- Take one recovery or preparation step with a hopeful mindset.

- Replace a negative expectation with a truth from Jeremiah 29:11.

- Thank God for plans that include hope and a future beyond this season.

Quiet Prayer: Heavenly Lord, thank You for steadying me when I feel hopeless. Help me trust Your plans when fear and disappointment linger. Renew my confidence as I heal and move forward. Teach me to expect good again as I place my faith fully in You. **Amen.**

JOURNALING & NOTES

25

CONFIDENCE FOR THE FUTURE

"Those who hope in the Lord will renew their strength. They will soar on wings like eagles; they will run and not grow weary, they will walk and not be faint."
Isaiah 40:31

Scripture Insight: Isaiah 40:31 speaks to renewal that comes from hope placed in the Lord rather than in circumstances. Strength is not described as self-generated or forced. It is renewed through trust. Waiting on God does not weaken believers. It restores endurance for what lies ahead.

For injured athletes, the future can feel uncertain and intimidating. Strength may feel depleted after pain, setbacks, or long recovery. This Scripture reminds us that hope fuels renewal. God restores strength not only for today's demands but for what is coming next. When an athlete anchors hope in the Lord, endurance returns gradually, preparing both body and spirit for the future ahead.

TESTED ON THE SIDELINES

Athlete Spotlight: Michael Chang faced physical challenges that tested endurance later in his tennis career. Injuries and physical strain disrupted momentum and limited consistency. Persistent hip problems, including damage that required surgery in the late

1990s, affected his movement and stamina on the tennis court. Recovery required patience as strength and stamina had to be rebuilt carefully over time.

For a player known for speed and persistence, physical limitation challenged his core identity. Training demanded restraint and focus rather than intensity alone. Preparing for the future meant accepting that his strength and endurance would return gradually, not instantly.

As his body required greater care, Chang learned to pace his preparation differently, accepting slower gains in exchange for longevity. Expectations shifted from immediate outcomes to sustainable progress. Faith provided steadiness when confidence in the process could not be measured by results alone. Chang's internal strength was rebuilt through steady effort and trust in the Lord rather than urgency.

Those seasons reinforced the promise of Isaiah 40. Hope placed in the Lord renewed endurance. Strength returned in time, equipping him for what came next. Chang's experience reflects the truth that waiting with faith prepares athletes not just for recovery, but for a future beyond it.

CHAMPION YOUR FAITH

Personal Reflection: Injury can make the return to your sport feel distant or uncertain. You may wonder whether strength, confidence, or opportunities will return. Hope rooted in God changes how you view what lies ahead. Like Michael, you may be learning that renewal takes time. God restores strength steadily as you trust Him. The future is not something to fear when hope remains anchored in the Lord.

Reflection Questions: *What concerns do I have about my future right now? Where do I feel weakest or most uncertain in my recovery? How does placing hope in God affect my outlook?*

Faith in Action:

- Identify one worry about your return to your sport and

place it intentionally in God's care today.

- Choose a single action today that moves your body and mindset forward.

- Encourage yourself by recalling a time when endurance was restored after difficulty.

- Thank God for renewing hope and strength even when progress feels gradual.

Quiet Prayer: Everlasting Father, thank You for renewing my strength as I place my hope in You. Help me trust You with my future when the uncertainty of my return weighs me down. Restore my endurance step by step as I continue healing. Prepare me for what lies ahead as I wait faithfully in Your care. **Amen.**

JOURNALING & NOTES

CHAPTER 6: TEAM IMPACT & INFLUENCE

Supporting, Leading & Serving While Injured

26

STILL PART OF THE TEAM

"Just as a body, though one, has many parts, but all its many parts form one body, so it is with Christ."
1 Corinthians 12:12

Scripture Insight: 1 Corinthians 12 tells us that unity does not depend on visibility or role. Every part of the body matters, even when some parts are less seen than others. Value comes from belonging, not from position. Being part of the body means contributing in different ways at different times.

Injury often makes athletes feel removed from their team. Reduced minutes, sidelined roles, or distance from competition can create a sense of disconnection. This Scripture speaks directly to that fear. Even when an athlete is not competing, they remain part of the body. God does not measure value by activity level. He affirms belonging regardless of role, reminding injured athletes that presence still matters and purpose remains intact.

TESTED ON THE SIDELINES

Athlete Spotlight: Benjamin Watson is an NFL tight end whose role shifted dramatically after a torn Achilles tendon in 2010 ended his season and required months of rehabilitation. While recovering, he was forced to contribute from the sidelines rather than on the field, learning to encourage teammates and stay engaged even when he physically could not participate. Remaining part of the team required patience, humility, and purpose beyond playing time.

Rather than withdrawing, Watson leaned into leadership and encouragement. Even while sidelined, he remained engaged with his teammates, offering guidance and support. His influence and impact on the team did not disappear because his role changed. It adapted.

Faith shaped his perspective. Watson understood that his contribution was not limited to playing time. He remained committed to serving the team wherever he was needed. Injury became a season to lead and influence differently rather than disengage.

That mindset reflected the truth of 1 Corinthians 12. Watson remained part of the team because belonging does not depend on physical readiness alone. His presence, character, and influence proved that purpose remains even when roles change.

CHAMPION YOUR FAITH

Personal Reflection: Being sidelined can make you feel disconnected from your teammates or overlooked. You may wonder whether you still matter to your team. 1 Corinthians 12 reminds us that belonging does not disappear when roles shift. Like Benjamin, you may be learning that contribution looks different in a season of injury. God values your presence and influence even when participation is limited. You are still part of the team.

Reflection Questions: *Where do I feel disconnected from my team right now? How has injury changed the way I see my role? What strengths can I still offer even while I am recovering? How does knowing I still belong affect my mindset?*

Faith in Action:

- Identify one way you can encourage or influence a teammate today.

- Stay engaged with your team by attending team practices and games.

- Replace feelings of isolation with intentional connection by encouraging and mentoring teammates.

- Thank God for placing you within a team that values every role.

Quiet Prayer: God, thank You, for reminding me that I still belong in my sport. Help me see my value even when my role looks different. Teach me to serve faithfully wherever I am placed. Strengthen my heart as I remain connected and supportive during this season. **Amen.**

JOURNALING & NOTES

27

LEADING FROM THE SIDELINES

"For even the Son of Man did not come to be served, but to serve, and to give His life as a ransom for many."
Mark 10:45

Scripture Insight: Mark 10:45 redefines leadership. Jesus teaches that true influence is not rooted in position, visibility, or control. It is expressed through service. Leadership is measured by willingness to help others, not by recognition or authority. Serving reflects strength shaped by humility.

For injured athletes, leadership can feel paused when playing time disappears. Being sidelined may create doubt about usefulness or impact. This Scripture reminds us that leadership does not stop when participation changes. God values service in every form. Choosing to serve teammates through encouragement, presence, and support reflects Christ-like leadership, even when competition is temporarily out of reach.

TESTED ON THE SIDELINES

Athlete Spotlight: Candace Parker is a WNBA champion and former league MVP whose role shifted during the 2019 season after a shoulder injury required surgery, limiting her availability with the Los Angeles Sparks. Watching from the sidelines tested her mental strength and self-identity. Extended time away from the court forced her to contribute through leadership, communication, and presence rather than minutes played.

Rather than disengaging, Parker remained actively invested in her team. She offered insight, encouragement, and leadership during practices and games. Her valuable experience allowed her to support teammates through communication and example.

Parker soon understood that leadership and influence is not limited to physical presence on the court. Serving teammates became an opportunity rather than a setback. She chose to invest in the team's success regardless of her injury and personal circumstances.

That approach reflects the message of Mark 10. Leadership rooted in service remains powerful even when visibility on the court decreases. By leading from the sidelines, Parker demonstrated that influence is sustained through humility, commitment, and faith-filled service.

CHAMPION YOUR FAITH

Personal Reflection: Being sidelined can make leadership feel out of reach. You may wonder how to contribute when you are not actively competing. God calls you to serve wherever you are placed on your team. Influence grows when you invest in others, even from the sidelines.

Reflection Questions: *How has this injury changed my view of leadership? Where can I serve my team even without playing? What attitudes help me lead with humility and character? How does serving others strengthen my faith?*

Faith in Action:

- Look for one opportunity to encourage or support a teammate today.

- Stay mentally engaged on your team by observing and mentoring during practices or games.

- Choose humility by celebrating others' success without comparison.

- Thank God for opportunities to lead through service.

Quiet Prayer: Lord, thank You for showing me what true leadership looks like. Help me serve faithfully on my team even when my role looks different. Teach me to lead by Your example with humility and grace. Use my presence to encourage others as I trust You in this season. **Amen.**

JOURNALING & NOTES

28

ENCOURING OTHERS THROUGH YOUR EXAMPLE

"And let us consider how we may spur one another on toward love and good deeds, not giving up meeting together, as some are in the habit of doing, but encouraging one another."
Hebrews 10:24–25

Scripture Insight: Hebrews 10:24–25 tells us that faith is meant to be lived out in community, and calls us to think about how our actions affect others and to use our presence to strengthen those around us. Encouragement helps faith stay active, especially during difficult seasons.

An injury can make athletes feel less useful to their team. When physical contribution is limited, influence may feel diminished. Injured athletes still have the ability to encourage, support, and inspire others through attitude and example. God uses presence, words, and example to build others up. Encouragement offered during hardship often carries greater weight because it reflects faith lived out, not just spoken.

TESTED ON THE SIDELINES

Athlete Spotlight: Julie Ertz is a World Cup–winning US Women's National Team midfielder who saw her role shift during the 2018 season after a knee injury (MCL tear) that pulled her off the field. Time away from full competition moved her influence from constant on-field presence to leadership through communication, encouragement, and service. Recovery required patience and mental discipline as she rebuilt strength while staying fully invested in her team.

Even while sidelined, Ertz remained engaged with teammates. Her intensity, preparation, and focus did not disappear because playing time changed. She continued to model discipline through rehabilitation and practice habits. Teammates watched how she responded to setbacks and uncertainty.

Faith influenced her consistency. Ertz understood that leadership through example speaks louder than instruction. Showing up prepared, staying positive, and remaining committed to her teammates sent a message of perseverance and trust. Encouragement flowed naturally through her actions rather than words alone. Julie's influence strengthened her team culture. By choosing to lead through example during injury, Ertz reflected the message of Hebrews 10. Encouragement rooted in action inspires others toward faithfulness, commitment, and effort even during challenging seasons.

CHAMPION YOUR FAITH

Personal Reflection: Injury can make you feel like your impact on your team is reduced. You may wonder if others still notice your effort or attitude. Scripture reminds us that encouragement to others often carries the most weight when it is lived out quietly. Like Julie, you may be learning that your example still matters. God uses consistency, presence, and character to strengthen others, even when your role looks different.

Reflection Questions: *How does my attitude affect those around me during my recovery? Where can my example encourage others right now? How can I stay engaged with my team despite limitations?*

Faith in Action:

- Choose one habit today that reflects discipline and faithfulness.

- Offer encouragement and leadership to teammates through actions rather than words.

- Stay present and supportive during team practices and games.

- Thank God for opportunities to influence and lead others through your example.

Quiet Prayer: Thank You, Heavenly Father, for allowing my life to encourage others even when my role has changed. Help me live out my faith through leadership and character. Teach me to strengthen those around me through my example. Use my actions to reflect Your love and faithfulness. **Amen.**

JOURNALING & NOTES

29

PURPOSE BEYOND PLAYING TIME

"For we are God's handiwork, created in Christ Jesus to do good works, which God prepared in advance for us to do."
Ephesians 2:10

Scripture Insight: Ephesians 2:10 reminds us that purpose is designed by God, not earned through performance. Our value comes from being created intentionally by Him. Good works are prepared in advance, meaning purpose exists before opportunity, visibility, or success. Identity is rooted in who God created us to be, not in what we accomplish.

For injured athletes, reduced playing time can shake confidence and identity. When minutes disappear, purpose can feel distant. This Scripture speaks directly to that fear. God's plans do not pause when participation changes. Purpose continues beyond the field, court, or track. Even during recovery, God is shaping your character, influence, and impact. Playing time may change, but God's calling does not.

TESTED ON THE SIDELINES

Athlete Spotlight: Paul Rabil is a professional lacrosse midfielder and one of the most influential players in the sport's history. During the 2013 season, a significant ankle injury that required surgery disrupted his availability and rhythm, forcing extended recovery and limiting his ability to play at full speed. Time away from peak competition challenged his routine and tested his patience. Reduced playing time created moments where identity and direction required reflection.

Rather than measuring value by minutes played, Rabil focused more on leadership and growth. He stayed engaged through practices, mentoring, and contributing in ways that extended beyond personal statistics. His purpose was expressed through influence and service rather than visibility alone.

Paul's faith in God shaped his understanding of him impact on the team. Rabil recognized that purpose is not limited to being on the field. Leading, encouraging, and investing in others mattered just as much as competition. Injury became a season to grow in perspective rather than withdraw.

That mindset reflects Ephesians 2. Purpose extends beyond playing time. God's work continues even when roles shift. By embracing influence beyond performance, Rabil demonstrated that his purpose and calling remains steady, regardless of circumstances.

CHAMPION YOUR FAITH

Personal Reflection: Limited playing time can make your purpose feel diminished. You may wonder how you still fit in or matter. Scripture reminds us that purpose is not dependent on opportunity. Influence, growth, and character continue to matter deeply, even when participation is reduced.

Reflection Questions: *Where do I struggle to separate my purpose from playing time? How has injury affected how I see my value? What ways can I contribute beyond performance right now? How does knowing God designed my purpose change my perspective?*

Faith in Action:

- Identify one way you can serve or encourage teammates today.

- Invest in growth areas that do not depend on playing time.

- Remain diligent in preparation even when chances to compete are few.

- Thank God for purpose that extends beyond performance.

Quiet Prayer: Dear God, thank You for designing my purpose with intention and care. Help me trust that my value remains steady even when playing time changes. Open my eyes to ways I can serve my teammates and grow during this season. Teach me to walk confidently in the purpose You prepared for me. **Amen.**

JOURNALING & NOTES

30

STRONGER TOGETHER

"Two are better than one, because they have a good return for their labor: If either of them falls down, one can help the other up."
Ecclesiastes 4:9–10

Scripture Insight: Ecclesiastes 4:9–10 emphasizes God's design for strength through connection. These verses do not deny that people will fall. They acknowledge it. What matters is that no one is meant to face hardship alone. God highlights the power of support, presence, and shared burden in moments of weakness.

Injury can tempt athletes toward isolation. Pain, frustration, and pride may push you to withdraw just when support is needed most. This Scripture reminds us that healing is not only physical. It is relational. God often provides strength through people who walk alongside us. Allowing others to help does not signal weakness. It reflects wisdom and trust in how God designed community to function.

TESTED ON THE SIDELINES

Athlete Spotlight: Albert Pujols is a future Hall of Fame Major League Baseball first baseman whose later seasons were shaped by chronic foot and plantar fasciitis issues, along with knee discomfort that limited mobility and endurance. Persistent pain made running, fielding, and daily preparation more demanding, forcing adjustments in his training, rest, and expectations. Competing at an elite level required managing discomfort rather than playing pain-free. Playing through this on-going discomfort demanded humility and reliance on others.

Pujols' recovery seasons shifted how he approached the game. Support from trainers, teammates, and coaches became essential. Leaning on others helped sustain him physically and mentally. Strength was no longer about carrying everything alone.

Albert's faith reinforced that dependence on other is not weakness. Allowing others to support him created stability, mentally and emotionally, during seasons of limitation.

Those last seasons for Pujols reflected the wisdom of Ecclesiastes. When one falls, another helps lift them up. Pujols' experience shows that strength grows when your burdens are shared. Healing, endurance, and purpose are sustained best together, not in isolation.

CHAMPION YOUR FAITH

Personal Reflection: Injury can make you feel alone, even when people are nearby. You may hesitate to ask for help or feel pressure to handle everything yourself. Ecclesiastes 4:9–10 reminds us that strength is multiplied through connection. God often works through people to provide encouragement, accountability, and strength when you need it most.

Reflection Questions: *Where am I tempted to isolate myself right now? Who has God placed around me to support my healing? What makes it hard for me to ask for help? How does trusting others strengthen my faith in God?*

Faith in Action:

- Reach out to one person and share honestly how you are doing.

- Accept support from your teammates and coaches rather than trying to carry everything alone.

- Encourage someone else who may also be struggling.

- Thank God for the people He has placed in your life.

Quiet Prayer: Everlasting Father, thank You for creating me to grow and heal within my team. Help me receive support with humility and offer encouragement freely to others. Remind me that I am not meant to walk this season alone. Strengthen my faith in You as I lean into the relationships You have given me. **Amen.**

JOURNALING & NOTES

READY FOR THE COMEBACK

If you are reading these final pages, you have endured some of the most difficult days you will face as an athlete, and you have not been defeated by it. Injury tested you physically, mentally, and emotionally. It forced you to slow down, adjust, refocus, and face parts of yourself that competition often distracts you from. And yet, you did not quit. You stayed faithful. You kept showing up in your recovery day after day.

This season asked more of you as an athlete than wins or statistics ever could. You learned how to trust God when progress felt slow. You learned how to stay disciplined when motivation was gone. You learned how to separate your identity from performance and your value from playing time. Those lessons did not weaken you. They strengthened your character in ways that will last long after you return to competition.

Through recovery, you rebuilt more than your body. You rebuilt confidence rooted in truth, not circumstances. You rebuilt faith that holds steady when schedules and timelines change. You rebuilt mental strength that does not collapse when pressure returns. You learned how to endure, how to lead, how to stay connected to your team, and how to believe again.

This season shaped you.

You are not returning as the same athlete you were before the injury. You are returning wiser, steadier, and more grounded. You know how to face adversity. You know how to wait without losing heart. You know how to trust God when outcomes are uncertain. Those qualities will serve you not only in your sport, but in every arena of life.

Your comeback is not just about physical readiness. It is about confidence restored. Faith strengthened. Purpose clarified. Whatever comes next, you are prepared for it. You have already proven you can endure through hardships and difficult days. You have already grown through the hardest part.

As you step forward, carry what this season gave you. Carry patience. Carry resilience. Carry trust. Let your recovery remind you of what you are capable of when faith leads the way.

You endured the injury.
You stayed faithful in recovery.
Your body may have been injured, but your spirit was strengthened.
Your confidence was rebuilt.

Your future as an athlete is still full of promise, and soon you will be ready for your big comeback.

TOP 15 POWER VERSES
Every Athlete Should Memorize

Every champion has a playbook. Every strong athlete of faith has verses they return to in moments of pressure, disappointment, doubt, and challenge. These 15 Scriptures are your spiritual "highlight reel" — short, powerful truths to carry into the locker room, onto the field, and into every part of your life. When pressure builds, when self-doubt creeps in, injury strikes, or when the world says you're not enough, these verses remind you who you are in Christ. Memorize them. Speak them. Live them.

1. Philippians 4:13 - "*I can do all things through Christ who strengthens me.*"
Pressure moments? This is your go-to. Your strength doesn't come from nerves, talent, or even preparation. It comes from Christ.

2. Matthew 19:26 - "*With God all things are possible.*"
A reminder that no obstacle is too big when God is involved and working on your behalf.

3. Romans 8:28 - "*And we know that in all things God works for the good of those who love him.*"
Even losses, injuries, and struggles can be used by God for a bigger purpose that you cannot yet see.

4. 1 Corinthians 16:13 - *"Be on your guard; stand firm in the faith; be courageous; be strong."*
In moments of pressure, fatigue, or uncertainty, this verse reminds you to stay mentally locked in. Strength is not only physical. Courage, focus, and faith keep you standing when things get hard.

5. Isaiah 40:31 - *"They will soar on wings like eagles; they will run and not grow weary."*
When you are tired, sore, or ready to quit, God is the one who renews your strength and lifts you forward.

6. Joshua 1:9 - *"Be strong and courageous. Do not be afraid; do not be discouraged, for the Lord your God will be with you wherever you go."*
Whether it is a big game, a tough tryout, or stepping into leadership, this verse reminds you that God is with you wherever you go.

7. Colossians 3:23 - *"Whatever you do, work at it with all your heart, as working for the Lord."*
AO1: Compete for an audience of one. God is your true and ultimate Coach in every season.

8. 2 Timothy 1:7 - *"For the Spirit God gave us does not make us timid, but gives us power, love and self-discipline."*
Confidence comes from God, not fear. Step onto the field with boldness, self-control, and trust.

9. Matthew 5:16 - *"Let your light shine before others, that they may see your good deeds and glorify your Father in heaven."*
Your witness matters more than your stat line. Let your effort, attitude, and character point others to God.

10. Romans 8:37 - *"In all these things we are more than conquerors through him who loved us."*
You are not just competing to survive. Through Christ, you already stand victorious.

11. Proverbs 3:5–6 - _"Trust in the Lord with all your heart and lean not on your own understanding; in all your ways submit to him, and he will make your paths straight."_
When life decisions, college choices, or uncertain seasons feel overwhelming, this verse reminds you that God directs the path of those who trust Him.

12. John 3:16 - _"For God so loved the world that he gave his one and only Son, that whoever believes in him shall not perish but have eternal life."_
The foundation of your faith is found here. Your worth is rooted in God's love, not in performance or achievement.

13. Isaiah 41:10 - _"So do not fear, for I am with you; do not be dismayed, for I am your God. I will strengthen you and help you; I will uphold you with my righteous right hand."_
When fear, nerves, or self-doubt rise, this verse reminds you that you never compete alone. God strengthens and upholds you.

14. Jeremiah 29:11 - _"For I know the plans I have for you,' declares the Lord, 'plans to prosper you and not to harm you, plans to give you hope and a future.'"_
For athletes worried about the next level, scholarships, or life beyond sports, this verse reminds you that God already has a plan for your future.

15. Isaiah 54:17 - _"No weapon forged against you will prevail, and you will refute every tongue that accuses you."_
Criticism, doubt, and opposition cannot stop what God has planned for your life. His purpose for you will stand.

Tape these verses in your locker. Write them on your shoes. Speak them before every game. They are more than words. They sharpen your focus, strengthen your resolve, and guide how you respond under pressure.

Other athletes memorize plays. You'll memorize truth. And that's what will make you unstoppable.

7 HABITS OF FAITH-DRIVEN ATHLETES

Talent may open doors, but habits build leaders and champions. The strongest athletes do not train their bodies alone. They train their faith with the same discipline. These seven habits are what set faith-driven athletes apart. If you live these out daily, you won't just be remembered for your stats. You'll be remembered as a legacy for Christ.

1. Pray Before You Compete

Bringing God into your preparation keeps pressure in its proper place. Even a brief prayer before practice or competition helps center your focus on trust rather than fear. Former NFL quarterback **Tim Tebow** was known for praying before games, not as a display, but as a reminder that faith comes before results, regardless of the stage.

2. Lead With Humility

True leadership is not about attention or status. It is about serving others well. Olympic swimmer **Katie Ledecky**, despite being one of the most accomplished athletes in history, consistently redirects credit away from herself and toward God. Humility keeps success from becoming a distraction and keeps faith at the center.

3. Bounce Back With Purpose

Setbacks, injuries, and mistakes are part of every athletic career. What matters is how you respond. Former NFL quarterback **Alex Smith** faced a devastating leg injury that threatened both his career and his health. Through patience, discipline, and faith, he returned to play, modeling perseverance and trust when the road back felt impossible.

4. Encourage Intentionally

Your words shape team culture more than you realize. Encouragement builds confidence, unity, and resilience. Former NFL quarterback **Drew Brees** was known not only for his leadership on the field, but for how consistently he lifted teammates during adversity. Faith-driven athletes use their voices to strengthen others.

5. Fuel Your Faith Daily

Just as your body needs regular training, your faith needs daily attention. World-record hurdler **Sydney McLaughlin-Levrone** openly shares how consistent time in Scripture helps her stay grounded under pressure. Faith grows through daily habits, not occasional moments.

6. Compete With Purpose

Statistics fade and trophies eventually gather dust, but competing for God's glory carries lasting meaning. Olympic volleyball champion **Kerri Walsh Jennings** has spoken about approaching competition with joy, gratitude, and faith, viewing each opportunity as a chance to honor God through effort and attitude.

7. Live Faith Beyond the Spotlight

Who you are away from competition matters just as much as how you perform. Former NBA star **Jeremy Lin** has consistently used his platform to speak about faith, humility, and identity in Christ, showing that influence does not depend on minutes played or headlines earned.

These habits are not about perfection. They are about consistency. When faith becomes part of how you train, compete, recover, and lead, it shapes who you become long after the final whistle.

Live these habits out consistently. Share them with teammates. Let your faith guide how you compete, recover, and respond under pressure. That is how athletes leave a legacy that lasts.

SCRIPTURE SOURCES

Throughout this devotional, Scripture passages are presented from a variety of Bible translations to enhance understanding and strengthen each message. The translations included are the New International Version (NIV), English Standard Version (ESV), and New Living Translation (NLT). These verses were thoughtfully selected to clearly convey biblical truth in a way that connects with athletes who are struggling with their injury and current recovery timeline. Used by permission. All rights reserved.

Biblica, Inc. (2011). *The Holy Bible: New International Version.* (Original work published 1973). Biblica, Inc.

Crossway. (2001). *The Holy Bible: English Standard Version.* Crossway Bibles.

Tyndale House Foundation. (2015). *The Holy Bible: New Living Translation.* (Original work published 1996). Tyndale House Publishers, Inc.

ATHLETE INDEX

(Alphabetical Order by Last Name)

SCRIPTURE INDEX
(Ordered by Book of the Bible)

Isaiah
43:1 — Still Chosen (Day 1) – Page 2
55:8–9 — When You Don't Understand the Plan (Day 4) – Page 11
40:31 — Confidence for the Future (Day 25) – Page 78

Jeremiah
29:11 — Expecting Good Again (Day 24) – Page 75

Lamentations
3:31–32 — Strength Built in Silence (Day 13) – Page 40

Habakkuk
2:3 — Hope When the Timeline Changes (Day 21) – Page 66

Micah
7:8 — Bouncing Back After Setbacks (Day 11) – Page 34

Psalms
27:14 — Faith on the Sidelines (Day 3) – Page 8
46:10 — Letting Go of Control (Day 5) – Page 14
34:19 — Rising from Disappointment (Day 15) – Page 46
37:23–24 — Trusting the Process (Day 20) – Page 62
42:11 — Light in the Dark Season (Day 22) – Page 69

9 781968 213084